EARLY INTERMEDIATE

The Blue Bird

7 Magical Piano Solos by Naoko Ikeda

Inspired by the Maurice Maeterlinck play

ISBN 978-1-5400-2559-3

EXCLUSIVELY DISTRIBUTED BY

WILLIS MUSIC

Hal•Leonard®

Visit Hal Leonard Online at
www.halleonard.com

Contact Us:
Hal Leonard
7777 West Bluemound Road
Milwaukee, WI 53213
Email: info@halleonard.com

In Europe contact:
Hal Leonard Europe Limited
Distribution Centre, Newmarket Road
Bury St Edmunds, Suffolk, IP33 3YB
Email: info@halleonardeurope.com

In Australia contact:
Hal Leonard Australia Pty. Ltd.
4 Lentara Court
Cheltenham, Victoria, 3192 Australia
Email: info@halleonard.com.au

For Yuri Masuko

Happiness
(Prologue)

It's a calm morning. The curtains flutter, a Blue Bird sings.

Naoko Ikeda

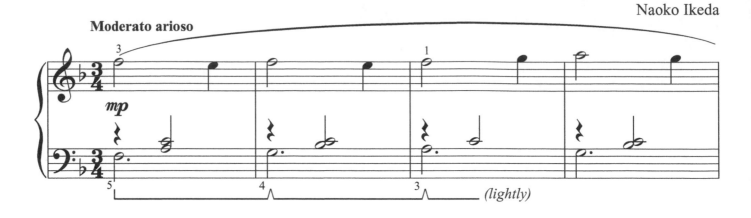

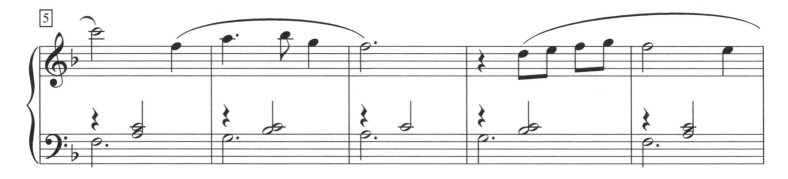

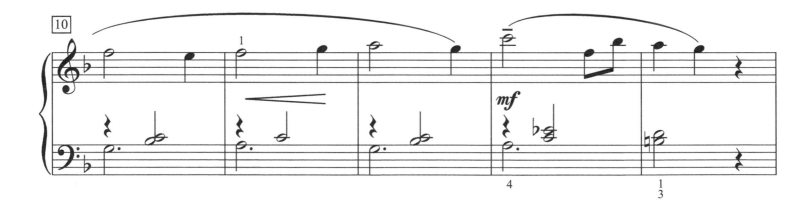

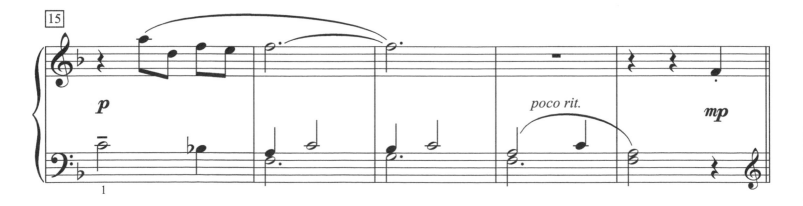

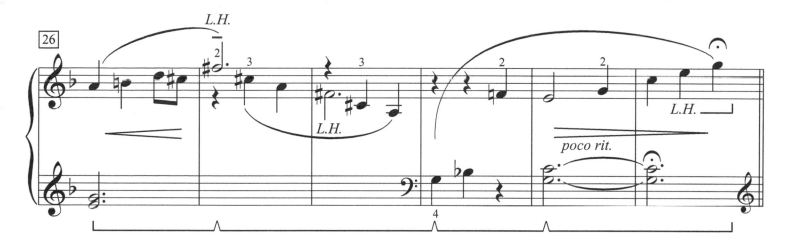

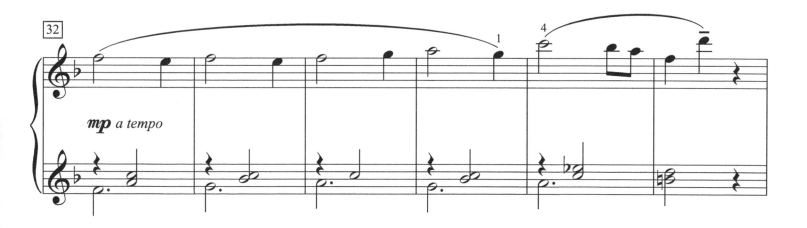

4

The Magic Forest

The seven dwarfs march happily into the magic forest to work. (It's where the Blue Bird lives.)

Naoko Ikeda

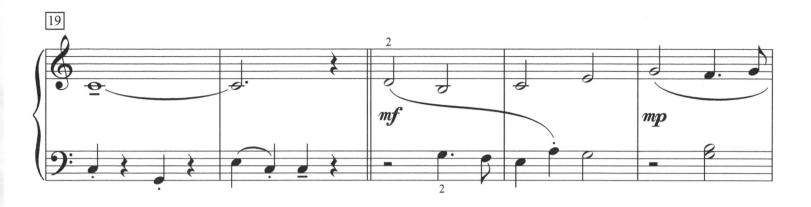

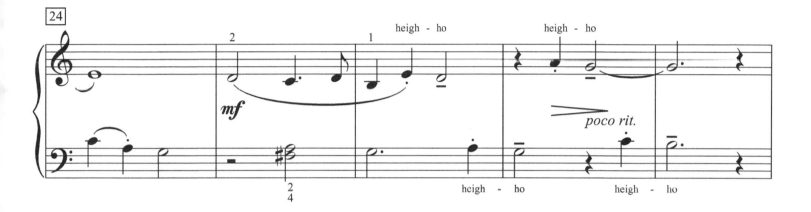

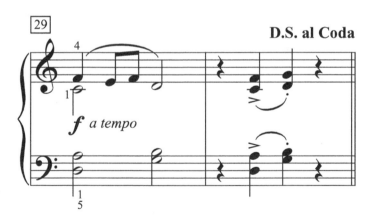

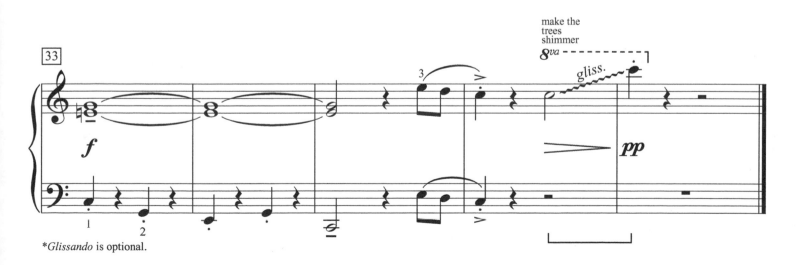

Glissando is optional.

Mysterious Wind

The trees of the forest rustle; it's a powerful, ruminating wind.

Naoko Ikeda

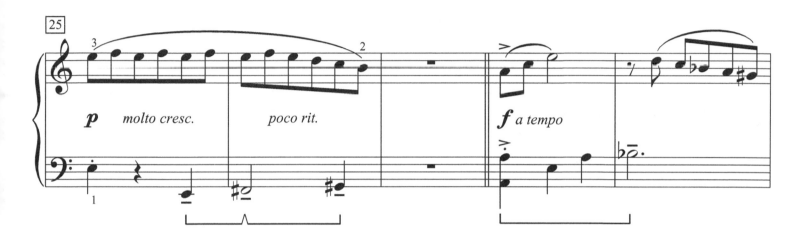

For Masae Nagasawa

Song of the Blue Bird

... a gentle melody that is only heard by those seeking true happiness.

Naoko Ikeda

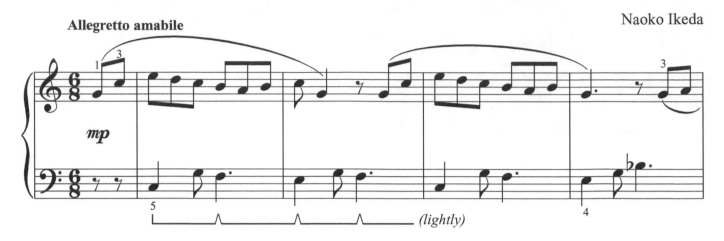

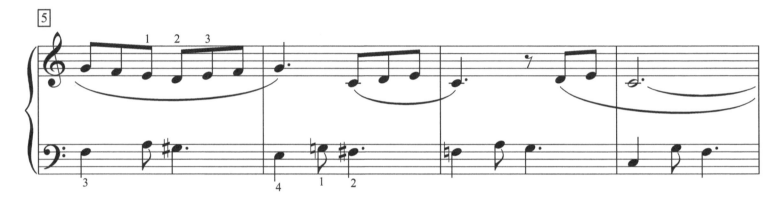

The White Rabbit

The White Rabbit screams: "I'm late! I'm late!! I'm late!!!"
Can he deliver the Blue Bird to the Queen of Hearts?

Naoko Ikeda

He hops...   and skips...

Dark Blue Night

The most beautiful moments happen at night. The fairytale is ending.

Naoko Ikeda

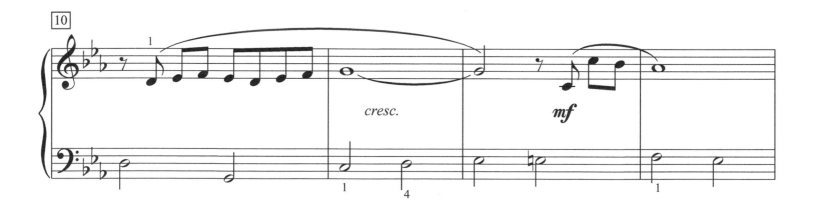

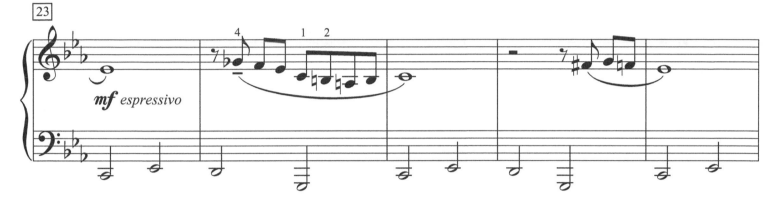

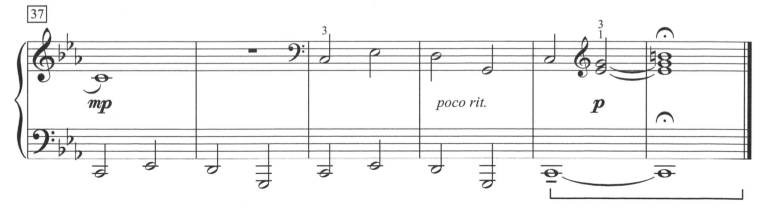

For Hiroko Yasuda

Happiness

(Epilogue)

"Happiness surrounds you every day," the Blue Bird observes, and flies away.

Naoko Ikeda

Andantino; calmly

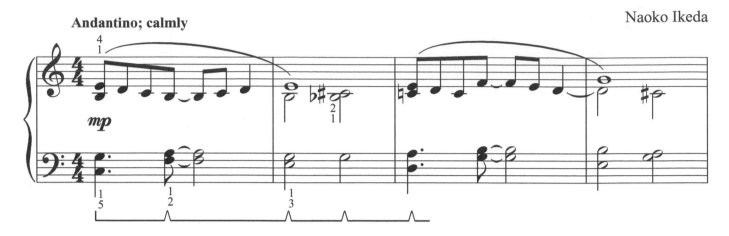

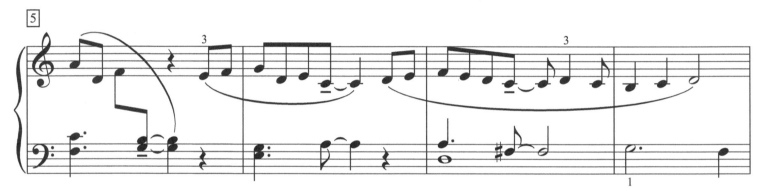

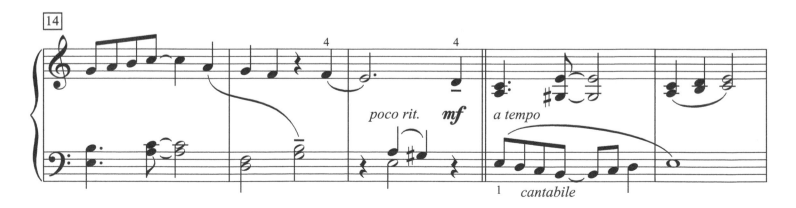

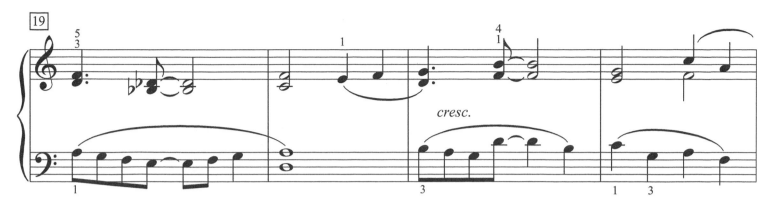

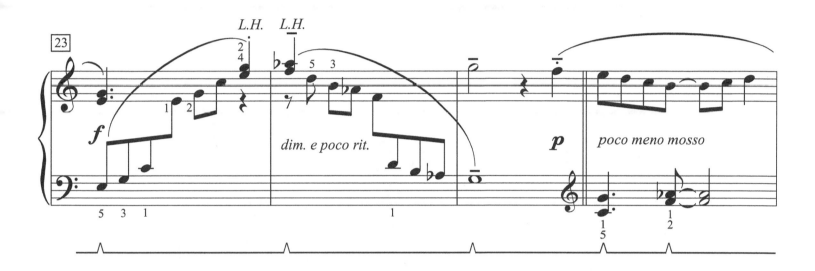

✦ Also by Naoko Ikeda ✦

AURORA • HL00196677 • Early to Mid-Intermediate

Five soulful solos "inspired by the northern sky, and in particular the Scandinavian landscapes of my own imagination," writes Naoko Ikeda. Introspective pieces, yet full of warmth.

TITLES:
Flora • Ethereal Summer • Land of the Midnight Sun • Aurora • A Sea of Clouds

Includes performance notes.